Scrapbooking

The Ultimate guide to Scrapbooking for Beginners in 30 Minutes or Less!

Copyright © 2015

All rights reserved. No part of this book may be reproduced in any form without permission in writing from the author. Reviewers may quote brief passages in reviews.

Disclaimer

No part of this publication may be reproduced or transmitted in any form or by any means, mechanical or electronic, including photocopying or recording, or by any information storage and retrieval system, or transmitted by email without permission in writing from the publisher.

While all attempts and efforts have been made to verify the information held within this publication, neither the author nor the publisher assumes any responsibility for errors, omissions, or opposing interpretations of the content herein.

This book is for entertainment purposes only. The views expressed are those of the author alone, and should not be taken as expert instruction or commands. The reader of this book is responsible for his or her own actions when it comes to reading the book.

Adherence to all applicable laws and regulations, including international, federal, state, and local governing professional licensing, business practices, advertising, and all other aspects of doing business in the US, Canada, or any other jurisdiction is the sole responsibility of the purchaser or reader.

Neither the author nor the publisher assumes any responsibility or liability whatsoever on the behalf of the purchaser or reader of these materials.

Any received slight of any individual or organization is purely unintentional.

Table of Contents

Introduction

Chapter 1 - The Beauty of Scrapbooking

Chapter 2 - Basic Supplies and Materials to Use

Chapter 3 - Let's Start Working

Chapter 4 - Creating Catchy Titles

Chapter 5 - The Layout Page

Chapter 6 - More Scrapbooking Tips

Conclusion

Bonus Chapter: Make Your Own Jewelry

Introduction

First and foremost I want to thank you for downloading the book, "Scrapbooking: *The Ultimate guide to Scrapbooking for Beginners in 30 Minutes or Less!*"

In this book you will learn how to create a scrapbook that looks professionally made but is actually budget-friendly.

For most scrapbookers, making a scrapbook is beneficial. Not only have they had the chance to share their photos in a creative way, it also acts as their de-stressing activity and at the same time, a fun hobby for the family.

From choosing the photos, to creating layouts and placing the embellishments, surely scrapbooking is a good way to bond with the family while at the same time, be able to preserve memories. Likewise, it can be a great gift for various events and special occasions.

This book will teach various techniques on how to properly layout your page and use available resources and embellishments around you. No need to break the bank as scrapbooking is an inexpensive hobby that you can do at your own convenience. On the contrary scrapbooking is not really difficult and time consuming if you are knowledgeable about its basics. Let's learn the beauty of scrapbooking together!

Thanks again for downloading this book, I hope you enjoy it!

Chapter 1

The Beauty of Scrapbooking

More than just a hobby, scrapbooking is some people's way of journaling, preserving memories and de-stressing. In essence, a scrapbook is just a decorated photo album holding precious memorabilia such as letters, photos, ticket, certificates and other important stuff to those who are making them.

Mostly a scrapbook is intended for family vacations, weddings, baby's first's movements (first crawl, first time to sit, first walk) and other special events. It is a fun and creative hobby that the whole family can enjoy.

No Skills Required

Scrapbooking could be really all about gathering those photos and putting all your designs, notes and accessories in an album where you want it to be seen and shared with other people. It does not also require experience or skills to come up with a beautiful scrapbook. Cutting, pasting and writing could do well for your scrapbook.

However, with all the photos, accessories and ideas you want to include in your scrapbook, this whole thing could be overwhelming making it appear a monumental task especially for beginners. That is why we are here to give you basic ideas and tips in scrapbooking.

Build the Scrapbook Page

Below are some tips on how you can make a basic scrapbook page. You could apply these on all the pages of the album or do some modifications depending on your taste and purpose.

Select the photos you want to use – this could be a tough task since we usually want to include all the pictures that we have during an out of town trip with the family or during the birthday celebration of a family member. Having a theme for the scrapbook will help you choose which photos to include. Now, think of the pages as a story book where you have to relay a story in each page.

Choose your layout – most of the scrapbook albums come in a double-page spread. You can choose an album with pre-layout matching your theme. There are also albums with blank pages and it's up to you how to put your photos on it. Make sure though that the pictures are not crowded in a single page to make way for other decorations.

Work on the common theme- again you have a theme to work with hence, the photos, captions and other accessories should relative with the theme.

Before gluing all your elements such as embellishments, photos, stickers and notes on your paper, arrange them first and see if the page won't look crowded. As a rule of thumb, the center of the page should be the center of attraction as well. For overlapping elements, visually connect each piece for a neat arrangement.

Say something – others opt to handwritten dates, notes or names on the page while some wanted it computerized. Whichever way you want, be sure to make it nice and smooth. You can add embellishments as well to your words.

Have it the Freestyle Way

You can also download various templates, thought catalogs, headlines, cards or alphabet tiles online for free! Whilst many beginners tend to struggle in starting their scrapbooks, it is still considered one of the popular craft and hobby today. It can take many forms which makes it convenient for scrapbookers. You can use any materials you want, there are no rules to follow and you can take inspiration from others works.

Remember, there is no right or wrong when creating your scrapbook as long as it sticks with the theme and things can be easily identified. All you need is a little creativity in relaying your memories and stories through your journal and photos. You can also write the emotions, mood and thoughts that surround the picture such as "enjoying the white sands", or "baby and his first times".

Chapter 2

Basic Supplies and Materials to Use

Another good thing about making a scrapbook is that, you don't actually need to have a huge investment. An inexpensive or used album sheets or colored papers, scissors, glue, adhesives, patterned papers, cut-out letters from magazines and your photos can turn out to be extremely good when done.

You can have these supplies at any craft supply stores and school supplies shops. Some can already be present in your cabinets, garage, sewing kit or kitchen. Try looking in your kids' stuff and you'll surely find gems to use.

Some dos and don'ts in Using Adhesives and Glue

- To glue lightweight materials, use quality glue stick. Cheaper glue sticks tend to form small lumps on the material. These also can hold very few amount of glue and can dry up fast. When working with it, make sure that the surface is smooth otherwise; the paper can be torn in the process.

- Do not use hot glue for your photos. Whilst hot glue is strong, the acid and heat can damage the photos in the long run.

- Double-sided tapes are best in adhering photo frames, journaling shapes and die cuts to your layout. Make sure that it is acid-free and is especially designed for scrapbooking.

The Right Embellishments

Even if doing all these stuff sounds fun and exciting, it can be also stressful especially if you want to incorporate lots of things! Dozens of embellishments, numerous accessories and designs can be confusing hence, below are the most useful to use in almost all sorts of scrapbook themes.

Stickers - who wouldn't say no to themed stickers, border stickers, word or letter stickers and other variations of it? Surely, stickers are very handy, inexpensive and most useful embellishment you can use in your scrapbook. It can add personal and creative touch to your pages and can help pull your chosen theme together.

Chipboard letters - aside from letter stickers, these chipboard letters can do wonders in your title page, a heading or names of people or places in your scrapbook. You can buy these at craft stores at very affordable price or you can make your own by tracing letters in a patterned paper and cut it out. If you choose to buy it, plain letters are good options since you can always decorate or paint it according to your theme.

Paper punches - these come in various shapes, designs and sizes. You can have ornaments, stars, leaves, flowers, hearts, dogs, balls or gadgets and many other designs. Likewise, paper punches have plenty of uses;

OVERLAY - This is good for creating scrapbook with cards. The cut-outs can also be used as borders for the page.

OBJECTS - several patterns can be created with your cut-outs. You can search the internet for inspirations or do your own.

CONFETTI- another creative use of cut-outs is to use them as confetti for the page.

Brads and sequins - you can have assorted color of brads and sequins to add with your other embellishments. It offers dimension to a plain sticker or gives added attraction to your whole page.

Twine and ribbons- I believe that most scrap bookers love to use ribbons and twines in their scrapbook page. You can use these embellishments in so many ways; as border of the entire page, border of a photo, as a special accent especially for vintage theme or to create an image or object.

These embellishments can turn a plain scrapbook page in a fun, exciting and creative one. You don't really need to buy these materials as you can found similar items at home. Buttons, old ribbons, embellishments from your old dresses and decorative magazine covers can go a very long way. S more fulfilling and

Likewise, scrapbooking is more fulfilling and enjoyable if all your materials are in an easy-to-access place and come handy. You are becoming more productive, creative and flexible. If there are shelves available, make a list on how you may want to use it such as putting paper organizer, storage containers and other important stuffs for your scrapbooking activity.

What Album to Use

The most common size of album used for scrapbooking are 8 ½x11 and 12x12. However you can use whatever page size you like.

Binding type – is one of the popular choices since it allows the person to add or remove pages. Among the types are strap hinge, post-bound and ring binders. You can also use spiral bounds but it limits the ability to modify the pages.

Page protectors – most albums have standard page protectors but you can also buy separate protectors. It makes easier to slide memorabilia and photos into page protectors hence you can quickly make a scrapbook with minimum number of pages and embellishments.

Watch out for online suppliers that offer discounts on their scrapbook tools and supplies. Likewise, buying in wholesale can also give your discounts. And because there are plenty of suppliers in the market nowadays, find one that sells cheaper compared with other suppliers. Usually local craft stores provide inexpensive materials than the books or specialty stores.

I wouldn't be surprised if you want to use all the materials and supplies around but remember, too much of anything can be bad. Instead of adding more and more decor and embellishments in a single page, how about adding more pages? Be selective in what to use and what to include in your album as these can have an impact on your scrapbook goal. In time you will be able to create more interesting and wonderful scrapbook projects.

Chapter 3

Let's Start Working

Nonetheless, making a scrapbook is very easy and fun and just like any other "art work", there are simple things to do before we actually start working with our masterpiece.

Set up your workspace - those who are into scrapbooks for so long will agree that their most frustration is keeping their workspace clean and neat and at the same time, workable. Hence, you can't use your dining area as your work area or you will just find it difficult to finish the album without getting interrupted.

Your area doesn't need to be huge. You can actually use a small closet, the side of the basements or attic without stuffs or the top of the stair as long as it can be dedicated for your activity. Create an organizer or a box to keepsake all your materials as well.

Gather your materials and supplies- check the house or your cabinets for possible supplies such as markers, glue, scissors, decorative papers and paper trimmers. It's tempting to purchase various materials at the craft stores but it is always advisable to stick with the basics.

Collect materials that are related with your theme. For an instance, the theme is graduation hence, you can use the parent and graduate ribbons and the tickets or invitation to be included in your layout.

Set aside the photos to use – this part can be difficult especially if you want more photos than what the scrapbook can accommodate. Hence, choose the best photos in terms of focus and lighting. Discard the blurry and dark ones. Smiling photos are good but there are other photos that can best depict your theme or goal. If the scrapbook is intended for a wedding, instead of just using photos with the smiling groom and bride, include pictures of the wedding rings, the bride's shoes or the newlywed's hands.

Determine your scrapbook style – you can make your scrapbook look sophisticated or elegant. You can also make it fun and wacky. It all depends on the style or approach you want to express in your scrapbook. The style will also help you determine what kind of layout, theme and embellishments to use.

Designing the page - after the preliminaries, here comes the fun part of scrapbooking. You already have your workplace, materials and supplies to use and photos to include; deciding what layout and design to use will be the next focus.

The first page of course should be the title page but we will do it last so that the title will truly reflects the theme and the essence of your album. Star with the next two pages (spreads). Instead of thinking the page as separate units, make it a single spread that will capture related photos. Temporarily arrange the chosen pictures and find the best pattern that will also fit the theme.

You can trim the photos with a square or an oval template or make a frame per photo. Put your embellishments such as confetti, cut-outs, stickers and other decors but just make sure that won't overdo it. If you have plenty of photos to include, trim them down or use collage apps to save you from editing and printing.

Everything is really up to your taste and preference. Even if you are that not creative, many ideas are available online so try to use them as inspiration.

Start your journal - this is your chance to say something about the photo and the experience as a whole. This is one of the benefits of scrapbooking. You can help the readers to determine who is in your photos, where the picture was taken or what is the event. Use key phrases in describing the pictures or witty captions.

After completing the spreads, proceed with the catchy title page. Include only one photo that will represent the theme of your scrapbook. Keep this page simple as much as possible so the readers and viewers can anticipate the contents of the following pages.

If you wanted your journaling to be a secret or it means too personal for you, you can keep it in private by sliding a cardboard or paper strip in a discreet pocket or lift-up flap. Pockets also add depth. You can create these pockets to insert postcards, tickets, small shells, travel brochure, charms and other memento in your page.

Make sure that you are using quality papers and album for your scrapbook. It doesn't have to be too much expensive. Choose products that are long lasting so your scrapbook will last for years.

As you go along with your scrapbook projects, you will learn new things and gain experience. You will also soon discover that this is a relaxing, fun and productive hobby that needs not to be expensive.

Experiment More

Experiment with your work and do not concentrate too much on avoiding mistake and ruining the page. It is normal for you to commit mistakes while still learning the art of scrapbooking. What matters is that you enjoy the entire process. Likewise, you don't have to scrapbook everything. Choose which memories you want to preserve in a scrapbook.

Most importantly, make sure that you complete one page of your scrapbook before starting a new page. One at a time so the pages will not end up incomplete or shallow. Remember that this scrapbook contains precious photos you would want to share with your friends and family. Take your time in finishing each page.

Chapter 4

Creating Catchy Titles

Beginners tend to be overwhelmed with the photos and various embellishments that they already forget to give importance with the title page. Remember that titles are as important as anything else you will put in your scrapbook. If you are lost and searching for ideas about making a catchy title page, below are some tips you can use.

Apply the KISS Principle

"Keep it simple, stupid" is a principle noted by U.S Navy back in the 60's. This recognizes the fact that things could be workable and effective when done simply rather than making it complex. In making your own scrapbook, KISS could mean keep it short and sweet or keep it simple and silly.

Instead of using long titles like "Our Vacation Last Summer", you can write "Summer Vacation" or "Last Summer" instead. The purpose of this is for you to say more during journaling on the pages of the scrapbook. Here you can fully explain and describe what is in the page. A one or two-word title could suffice and reflect the whole page. Likewise, you are enabling the readers to gain expectations and anticipation for the next spreads.

Use Locations

If you want, you can use the location or place where the pictures took place to be your title page. Instead of saying "Family Vacation" you can use "Beach" or the actual name of the resort or hotel you stayed in.

Big Bold or Subtle Italic

You can use various fonts, font colors and sizes with your title. Fortunately, there are plenty of free font generators online where you can create titles according to your theme. There are handwritten fonts as well that might look good with your homecoming theme.

Remember, the title can pull off the page layout and its contents together. It also serves as the center of your page and without an attractive title; the whole thing will seem unfinished. However, coming with a "working" title is a struggle for most beginners especially for certain events such as weddings or birthday. One can easily put the word "wedding" and call it done but you can make it more interesting instead of using a very obvious title.

Date and Time

You can come up with dozens of interesting titles. If you are into a certain date or era, try to look for a specific word that will describe that era and your photo. Also, choose titles in relation with family, love, relationships and dreams. For random pictures, you can use generic titles but still give it more character. Do not focus entirely on the title. As you go on with your scrapbooking, you will eventually think of the best title for your work.

The title page highlights, suggests or summarizes the theme and the photos in your scrapbook layout. You can use simple phrases, quotes or sayings and names for your title page.

Perhaps, you don't want to have the title at the top of the page so try placing it anywhere as long as it's noticeable and readable. You may handwrite your title or use stamps, stencils, computer-generated fonts, and acrylic paint and alphabet stickers. Mix and match these ideas to come up with an awesome title page.

Chapter 5

The Layout Page

Contrary on what most of us believe, a good layout is something that is well-constructed and well-thought. We don't really need to be experts in designs but having some basic knowledge and becoming familiar with fundamental elements of lay-outing will have a huge impact on your scrapbook as a whole. You can also come up with your own style.

If you hear of the word scrap lifter, this term refers to new scrapbookers who scrap lift or sees other beautiful layouts and designs as inspiration for their work. They may get it from magazines, online designs or in other scrapbooks and copied it with their own photos and materials. This approach can create an interesting layout and page.

As you copy other's layout, you are also doing modifications with the materials you have hence; you will eventually learn how to complete the layout on your own. This will also help you find out your own preference when it comes to layout and designs. Moreover, focus on the things you want your scrapbook to be. There are no boundaries with what you can do with your scrapbook.

Standard Elements

Floor plan - is one of a sketch layout that will help you see the structure of a basic layout. The photos and other materials you will use will determine the finish look of your scrapbook. In floor plans, only the simple embellishments can be seen and not the detailed ones.

Background - this is where the layout starts. The way you put this foundation can have a significant impact on your layout style. Likewise, your background serves as the anchor for your photos, embellishments and journal. It will help you attract your readers or viewers to look at your photos. The color of the background can also affect the outcome of your page.

Borders – this usually add appeal to your photo or the page where you place it. Decorative borders can be made of embellishments, cut-outs, texts or ribbons. You can also use charms, tags, colored papers and small metal to design the border but be sure that it has connection with the theme and photos included.

The borders can also be referred as photo corners that intend to add more character and to make the photo outstanding.

Photo Mat – this refers to the layer underneath the photo, leaving it with an all-around border. It helps in making the photo standout. Your mat can be made of patterned paper, cardstock, acrylic paint and other decorative elements. You can also have it thick, thin, flat, dimensional, plain or with accents depending on the effect you desire. However you don't actually need to mat all the photos in a page but only the focal-point ones.

Page accent – this can include flower, fabric, buttons, eyelets, stickers, brads or ribbons and anything that can enhance the layouts overall look. The accents should also support your theme but not too overwhelming that it attracts the viewers' attention more than the photos in the page.

Now that you already know the basic of lay-outing your photos, you can start making your own. You can also take advantage of downloadable E-Cuts. These are printable layouts and designs for you to enjoy. Consider the size of your page and album in choosing the best layout for your scrapbook.

Likewise, before actually gluing all your materials, make sure that you arrange them on the background accordingly.

Selecting Photos

The number of photos and their sizes will affect your layout plans. Likewise, the photos should be based on your theme as each page of the scrapbook has to tell a story. Most of the layouts are done in a double-page spread so if consider this when choosing the photos to include. You may choose to put a very special picture in the middle of a page or 3-4 photos to fit per page. Whichever layout you choose, be sure that the page is not overcrowded since you will be adding some embellishments.

If the photos just won't work with a double-age spread, a single page will do. There's no right or wrong layout so work freely with the photos and materials you have rather than focusing on covering the whole page. Select the pictures that look good together or have connection to each other. This will help you establish the story and your theme.

Chapter 6

More Scrapbooking Tips

Now that you are already equipped with the basics of scrapbooking, we will share with you other tips and techniques to enhance your skills and your future scrapbook projects. Similarly, these tips will save you time, money and other resources while achieving positive results with your projects.

Find inspiration – before, scrapbooking magazines and books were the only sources of inspirations for techniques, layouts and page ideas. Fortunately we have thousands of dedicated websites where we can get endless ideas, free templates, printables and other stuff that we can use in our scrapbook. Moreover, materials and supplies cannot only be found in thrift shops and office supplies stores since you can order online especially for rare finds.

Manufacturer's sites and design blogs are very helpful as well if you don't know how to use certain scrapbooking tools. The internet is also flourished with how-to-videos and tutorials for various themes. Literally, the inspiration for your scrapbook is endless. You can also join an online community and get tips and techniques from fellow scrapbookers and bloggers.

Added visual appeal – a good background can catch the viewer's attention. Select a background that will create visual interest such as a large curved shape cut-out from a patterned paper. You can also use plates, bowls or you r hands to draw these shapes.

Punches are another great stuff to use. These accents also help in creating interest. You can buy punches with various designs or do it on your own.

Sticker placement – stickers can make your page attractive or totally ruin it especially if you put in the wrong place and try to remove it. If you are using small stickers and paper punches, refrain from using too much of it to avoid clutter in your page. A large sticker will be more noticeable if you will outline it using a colored pen or patterned paper.

Another solution is to use waxed paper to cover a strip of cardboard where you can arrange and place your stickers to see if they look great on your page. Rearrange the pieces until you are satisfied with the outcome.

The right photos – your photos will tell your story thus, it is the essential part of any scrapbook layout. Choose the right photos to ensure the right flow of storytelling. Although "posed" pictures are usually used in scrapbooks or those that are taken professionally, candid shots are more fun and enticing to use. They tell more interesting stories than the posed ones. You can use unplanned photos with the posed one to come up with a nice tale.

Organize your ideas- apparently, scrapbooking is a way of de-stressing for some people but once in a while, they can experience "creative block". To combat this downfall and difficulty of getting fresh ideas, organize your scrapbook goals in a paper. Likewise, write down artistic ideas that you might think, read or heard somewhere during the day.

Organizing your supplies and materials will also help to ensure that you have all the things needed in your scrapbook. Not only in scrapbooking but being organize is an important factor for you to be productive in whatever it is you are doing. Secure a list of the essential things that you have to secure before starting with your project to avoid delay, frustrations and wastage.

Make use of other resources – aside from printed templates, cutouts and store-bought materials, newspaper clippings can also be added in your page. Moreover newspaper photos contain interesting stories and add character to your scrapbook. However, the paper used for these photos contain acid which can deteriorate the paper so preventive maintenance and care is a must.

You can preserve your newspaper clippings by mixing 1 tablet milk of magnesia and 1 quart of club soda. Dissolve the mixture completely and pour in a shallow pan. Lay the clippings in a flat pan and soak it in the mixture for a couple of hours. Carefully dry it with a soft towel. This can preserve the newspaper clippings for years.

Try scrapbooking kits – and because scrapbooking is becoming more popular nowadays, suppliers are also getting innovative. Instead of you purchasing separate items and materials for your scrapbook, there are scrapbook kits already available. These kits are usually intended to finish several pages.

Some comes with pre-printed templates, layouts and designs and all you have to do is to attach your photo. The kits also have a theme you can choose from. Make sure you are only buying quality scrapbooking kits since they are not all the same. These scrapbook kits are good for starters and for quick and easy page ideas. Even kids can enjoy scrapbooking as well. You can gain fresh ideas with these premade kits.

Keep things in control – although scrapbooking can be done with cheap materials, it can also get expensive in the long run especially if you cannot control the urge to buy embellishments, patterned papers, scrapbooking tools and other supplies that you believe are useful for you.

Keep on track and don't lose your control over your money in buying scrapbooking materials. You don't actually need to own every new tool. As much as possible work around your budget and be resourceful.

If you have a friend or relative that is also fond of scrapbooking you can both invest in a single tool which you can use or you will buy a certain tool and the other will go for another kind of tool. Perhaps, instead of buying premade templates try to create your own by using available stuffs.

Get advantage of the internet – if you have access to the internet well you have tons of scrapbook information available for free. Various websites offer free downloadables and printables. You can also get several ideas for your title page. There are also websites offering free fonts that are useful in your page.

Do not use everything - again, beginners usually start a bit frustrated with how their work turns out. They tend to use all the supplies, photos and materials they have on hand thinking that it would be best for their scrapbook. Well, it's not the case. Too much of these supplies will only make your page crowded and messy.

If you have tons of pictures to include, consider using accordion pages. This will allow you to fit in more photos and items in a single page without making it crowded.

Conclusion

Thank you again for downloading this book!

I hope this book was able to help you to get started preserving those memories in a very creative and fun way.

The next step upon successful completion of this book is to turn those plain photo albums into something unique and very useful scrapbook. Now that you know the basic supplies needed and you have some inspirations and ideas, my advice is to take things simple.

Beginners could feel overwhelmed by what they see in craft stores, online shops and magazines but don't fret! You can make a beautiful scrapbook by just using the things you already have at home plus a little creativity there. Definitely you will get the hang of it.

Moreover enjoy doing your scrapbook and learn from mistakes such as wrong placement stickers, untrimmed photos, messy handwriting or wrong use of ribbons and buttons. You will eventually learn how things work accordingly.

Pick old techniques and discover new ones and apply it together to come up with an extremely good scrapbook page. No right or wrong layouts or designs so feel free to explore other materials and layouts. Happy scrapping!

Finally, if you enjoyed this book, please take the time to share your thoughts and post a review on Amazon. It'd be greatly appreciated!

Thank you and good luck!

Bonus Chapter: Make Your Own Jewelry

Making Your Own Jewelry

Here are simple guidelines which can help you in your first project. Keep in mind that these are just suggestions and you have the option to change or adjust the pieces as you see fit.

1. Casual Bracelet

A casual bracelet is easy to make and it is ideal for those who want something unique and personalized to complement their outfits. Since the materials used for casual bracelets are not so expensive, you can also give the as gifts. This casual bracelet is so easy, you can even ask your kids to make it.

Start by preparing your materials. For this project, you need old buttons of different kinds and sizes. You can either look for old buttons you have at home or buy new buttons of different kinds. The more varied and colorful your buttons are, the better your necklace would look. Regular, two-hole buttons are perfect for this project. You will also need a fishing line or nylon to string together the buttons you've prepared.

Gauge the length of string that you would need for the bracelet. Make sure to give it allowance because you'll need to secure both ends of the bracelet. Start by inserting the fishing line up through one whole and down through the other. Continue doing this again and again until you reach the length you desire. Try to make sure that your design has a pattern. Apply the principles of design as you choose what buttons to include in your bracelet.

Make sure that the ends of the bracelet are secure. You can then add the clasp of your choice. Check and double-check everything to ensure that the clasps won't fall off. Try to ensure that the bracelet itself is sturdy as well. This is a great addition to everyday outfits! It would add charm, color and quirkiness to whatever you are planning to wear.

2. Bottle cap earrings

For another casual piece of jewelry, you can try making unique bottle cap earrings that will display your favorite contemporary beverages. If you have contemporary bottle caps, you can use those too. They are hip, attractive and very easy to do.

Start by preparing the materials you need. Have 2 matching bottle caps, 2 head pins, 2 ear wires and beads for design. As tools you'll need a small hammer, jewelry pliers and round-nose jewelry pliers. If you don't have these tools yet, try to be resourceful. Modify what you have with you in order to get the work done.

Don't work on a glass table. One of the first things that you should do is to make sure that the surface that you're working on is protected. Start by punching holes on the bottle caps. You can use this using a screwdriver, nail or AWL. Hammer the end of the screwdriver, nail or awl to the position where you want the hole to be. Be careful because the hammer could very easily hurt you.

Slip the head pin in the hole. Make sure that the pin is secure. The head of the pin should be inside the cap. You can then add the beads of your choice to the head pin. In effect, there would be something dangling that would make the earrings more attractive and colorful. Choose beads that match the color of your bottle cap. Also, make sure that you secure both ends of your pin so that the beads on your earrings won't fall off. You have the option to add as many holes as you can to add more beads or even a dangling chain. Play around with your materials and explore what you can do to give your work a unique and creative look.

Attach the ear wires and try on your earrings! Now you have a beautiful accessory and a nice conversation piece that will surely catch the eye of people around you.

3. Washer necklace

In this project, you can use washers to create a beautiful neck piece that will really catch the attention of people around you. Washers can be easily bought in hardware stores. By using your creativity, washers can be transformed into a beautiful necklace.

Start by preparing the materials you need. You'll need pliers, about ten washers or so (depending on how big and attractive you want your necklace to be); about twelve jump rings, a chain, and a bottle of nail polish in your favorite color. Lay down all your materials and get ready to work.

Start by painting one side of the washers and let dry. If you want, you can use different colors in painting the washers. You can even design them. It all depends on your personal style. Next, connect the washer to one another using the jump rings. You can form any shape you want. You can keep it simple or you can make it a bit more interesting. Currently, the trend is to wear V-shaped necklaces so you might want to consider making something like that. Play around with the washers until you come up with something which you think you will like.

Once you are happy with the way your washers are arranged, the next thing you can do is to attach the chain. Figure out which are the two ends of your washer arrangement. Connect each end of to the end of the chain to form the necklace. Adjust the length as needed.

Check the washers if any of them has chipped or cracked polish. Repaint them and let dry. If you want, you can top with a clear nail polish to give your painted washers additional protection.

CPSIA information can be obtained
at www.ICGtesting.com
Printed in the USA
BVHW031816250320
575981BV00001B/88